Building in Deeper Water

Building in Deeper Water

POEMS BY *Timothy Young*

THE THOUSANDS PRESS

Edited by Robert Bly

Cover art *The Wood Has Ears, the Field Has Eyes*, by Hieronymus Bosch

ISBN: 1-883070-05-8

Grateful acknowledgement is made to the editors of the following publications in which versions of some of these poems were printed earlier: *The Temple/El Templo*, *Mens Voices—A Quarterly*, *Potato Eyes*, *Pemmican #8*, *Northeast*, *Journal of Family Life*, *The Best American Poetry* 1999, *Loonfeather*, *The Blue Sofa Review*, *The Wolfhead Quarterly*, *Journal for Life*, *New Orleans Review*, *River Images*, *Farm Romance & Adventure*, *Poetry Motel*, *North Coast Review*, *Poetry*, *Free Verse*, and *Red Dragonfly Press*.

THE THOUSANDS PRESS

Distributed by Ally Press
524 Orleans Street, Saint Paul, Minnesota 55107
1 800 729 3002
http://www.catalog.com/ally/

In memory of my brother,
John Nicholas Young

Poems from Tough Wood
By Robert Bly

Some poets seem to strike off clean slabs of young wood with a carefree ease. We can tell that the poems grew fast, and there's not much strength to them. Tim Young's poems resemble boards with knots in them, boards too hard for knives sometimes, hard to unpack like knots in a rope, sometimes pulled tight. Marriages we all know are rich in knots, and he goes into his marriage that way.

"After the battle," he says to his wife, "you smile at me." Your love, he says, has been a long time withheld, and now it returns with the "fire of your hidden years."

> From knots and gnarled heartwood
> the fire burns hot and slow.
> Just as grief derives from struggling,
>
> and compassion is born from grief,
> the face of holiness returns with you,
> after the battle and the grief.

We can feel in this poem the longing that Frost sometimes expresses to enter the woods at the darkest place. He is determined not to avoid the sweat of difficulty, "the stain / Of tears . . . the sweet of bitter bark / And burning clove." Young says:

> Sometimes, in the middle of an argument, a door flies open,
> lightning flashes, and steely needles of rain begin to fall . . .
>
> Here, on the bluffs . . .
> we've had practice dealing with storms. . .
>
> If I have to carry a plywood sheet
> to nail over a broken window,
> I carry it knife-like into the wind,
> I walk sideways so the force won't throw me. . .
>
> I must resist the wind, just a bit,
> push against it, and yield slowly
> so we close the door together.

This is superb writing about relationship, and such writing is a rare gift among men. Besides relationships, there is also a man's friendship with the earth. He lived in the city, and moved to the country ten years ago. This man is able to bless nature. There's no rural sentimentality. There are poems about hunting, about the fox taking grouse, about beavers—just starting out—who build their first lodge too far from the deep water. The next time, they do it right

> having built
> in deeper water.

The writer is an adult man whose longing is still fresh:

> I'm leaning against an old oak
> beside a high meadow, still
> stalking the fawn of my desire,
> so that I might touch her fading spots.

There's a sweet poem about a cutout of an old woman's backside in a garden.

> This new country ritual shuns the bathtub Madonna
> for an elderly arse in the berries.

I'm glad to welcome this book into the community of poets. This book has a "lived life" in it, with poems for sons, fathers, grandfathers, even war. He recalls a time when he was a boy, watching a fight between two spiders. This poem attracted much attention during the recent Iraqi war:

> One spider limped on,
> with the other's head in its mouth.

> When I asked my mother about war,
> she told me, "You're thinking too much . . ."

> . . . I stood, between my mother
> and my father, thinking.

Contents

3.

1.

Still Stalking the Fawn

At this vulture perch over the river
a tiny oak has begun in humus
and already its small roots search
into the cracks of the limestone bluff.

I'm leaning against an old oak
beside a high meadow, still
stalking the fawn of my desire,
so that I might touch her fading spots.

Walking After Breakfast

Sometimes between the cardinal's first whistle
and the bee's morning hum,
a man hears the answer to a question
he forgot to ask.

The wet trunks of cedar trees
cross before me, like a bird's giant footprint.
Those lines are the map I saw
in the old branch library
where as a boy I read of herons,
and swans and great geese going north.

Whistling and humming at the same time
creates a third thing between my teeth
and I become a cricket singing
of spruce trees and nearby flies.
I taste both a cigar and coffee
and the question is—
how do I get on in life?

Having Flown

Having flown in dreams last night,
playfully, with the artistry
of a swallow through twilight,
I took up the saw this morning
and dropped the few trees
where the planned road will run.

Below the hill's crown,
and above the wet, willowy rut,
I piled brush for a squirrel cave
and a refuge for ruffed grouse.
From a mossy compost
I removed some old logs,
fitted now with fungus,
and threw them on the mound to dry.

When I threw one slippery log,
it knocked my head.
I guess a bit of sleep
remained in the log and me.
It wanted to remain in the must,
and I wanted to leave.

Sledgehammer

Once in awhile someone else guides my sledgehammer.
It happens when the air is chilled and quiet,
my arms weary, my trunk a warm sea of sweat,
and I forget I am of any world.

Into my emptiness he arrives.
The arc of the steel head draws true
and the wedge drives through the icy wood
which stops the tip just as it touches the earth.

The log splits so perfectly I can only marvel
at the beauty the firewood angel brings.
I'm excited and happy but on the next log
I drive the wedge six inches into the ground.

After Confession

On a Saturday evening
I returned from confession
with a heart as clean as I could know.
I crossed the park and headed home
and saw through a lighted window,
a naked girl, older than I,
emerging from her bath.

Shame, as cold as April nights,
fell onto my shoulders.
I so wanted to watch.
Had she turned off her light,
she could have seen me.
I wouldn't have hid,
nor been able,
for my awkward soul and quaking legs
fastened me to the concrete.

In a moment of habit and modesty,
she drew the shade and broke the spell.
I've never learned her given name
though I know her by one I chose.
So if you know her, tell her I, too, love her,
and I call to her by that name,
whenever I walk into the dark,
or in the quiet light of autumn.

A Black Pig's Head

Down the snowy, Deep Creek Road,
I walk at ease, past the limestone
outcroppings, the nettling white pines,
and a hedge of cast-off wire spools.

Then. . . in the ditch. . .
crows on a dead, black pig's head
pick at the eyes and cheeks,
the lips, the tongue and neck bone.

Tracks in the snow show a coyote
sniffed the fat and the bristle and left.
Vultures will come, as will the sun
and hawks, and dogs and mold.

When the weather turns there will be worms,
but for now, ice delays the rotting.
Somewhere nearby, in town
or at a farmhouse, pork is in the freezer.

It's always this way, I know. . .
the living kill to live, or eat the dead,
and these deeds go on and on
like the creek over stones to the sea.

In an Old Arm Chair

In an old arm chair I sit
drinking coffee and warming my feet
before the open cast iron stove.

Over the chimney a heavy wind
suddenly pulls the fire into
a roaring, hollow-filling horn blast.

My fears — the old, childish, and primal fears —
are sucked to the stove door, called
by a Bird-Faced One who demands my attention.

I lean toward the blaze and the heat
peels something from my face,
maybe another fear that feeds the Bird-Faced One

who rides the dark wind to the next fire.

Autumn Wind

When the wind turns
it creates a hole around which
leaves whirl. The current pulls
from nothing.

In a nail hole in the shed-siding
a whistle begins, as if the wind
and wood understood they were
just passing the cemetery.

I can't see what makes the whistle,
though I know the sound comes alive
because of what is missing.
So I blow on my hands
and over my thumbs to hoo
a beautiful hoo like an owl.

When Hunters Rise

When hunters rise, in the darkest hour,
every movement is a ceremony and relevant.
Stoke the banked coals. Eat a simple breakfast.
Gather rifles and sleep-scattered wits.
Step outside and breathe the cold air.
Let rituals warm the soul like long johns.

So few know this hour as well as hunters –
maybe monks, surely a prayerful shaman –
the hour before dawn when Someone Unnamed
walks the hospitals, the hotels and highway.
Even the criminal has finished his crimes for the night,
frightened by the Greatest Stalker.

But the hunter goes out with darkness in his weapon
rather than holding its stone in his heart.
He understands the fundament of life:
"something dies so another can live."
We know this because when the night goes to day,
the sun kills the stars in the sky.

A Grouse Died in a Fox's Mouth

Last night while I slept
a grouse died in a fox's mouth
on a snowy bridge.
This morning bloodied brown feathers
scatter toward the hills.

Silence absorbed the bird's last terrors,
the way the snow
holds tracks that come and go.
I step into that silence
where the grouse's screams
hang with a ripping feather coat,
where the fox's shadowy head
shakes hollow bird bones
that snap between her teeth
as a broody skull is crushed.

I see the fox track wind
over the hill to a den,
where kits are curled, waiting
for her raw red nipples
to feed them, again.

Two Dogs Bark in Far Away Trees

Two dogs bark in far away trees,
maybe the same woods where the old trapper
came upon a glowing oak,
burning from the inside without flames,
too hot to approach,
and more orange than the sun which was setting.

When he returned a week later
the blackened bark felt warm,
the inner fire still burned,
and he saw that in the woods
nothing else had changed.

When I prowl the woods
I wonder, "Is this the dead tree
that burned up inside?
Or is it that one above the rocks?
Or the one down in the gully?"

I Love the Single Deer Path

I love the single deer path
winding into wet, tangly night woods
where nocturnal squirrels,
and whip-poor-wills
usually fly tree-to-tree.

The Hunter walks from the known
to the not-known,
and water drops from leaf to leaf.
The humus grows moist,
still and womanly.

Beautiful Stars

What makes the stars so beautiful?
Their brilliant godlike fires?
At noon constellations glow
yet can't be seen from here.

In a cave darkness is darkness.
Yet when stars appear in darkness,
people see archers or dragons, or souls
who ride wild horses down the Milky Way.

Wild Plum

Maybe you pick a wild plum
from a wobbly ladder.
Go in between the thorns.
Part them for the fruit.

Then come down the ladder
before you taste
the sweet meat
and spit out the seed.

When all the plums are in
you can cook the flesh for jam
and dry the pits for a rattle.
But you still have to live with the thorns.

Beavers, Too Young

Beavers, who were too young,
built a lodge in the wrong place,
in the deep trees, under the forest spread
and much too near the highway.
The two of them cut the saplings properly
and wove a tight dome in high water.
Inside the dome three tunnels curled
up to the high dens where
they had matted grass for their comfort.

Then the flood receded.
They built again,
further out
among the cattails,
in deeper water.
They built again,
branch by branch,
a new lodge and home.

This is the way to live.
Dive into the swamp.
Emerge with a sweet root.
Then sit like a beaver
and enjoy your life,
having built
in deeper water.

2.

Puma Under a Mayan Blanket

I hear the purr of a great cat,
my wife under a Mayan blanket.

Your long, lithe body smells of water
and licked, clean hair.

The path of the puma crosses over you.
As I draw near, you retreat slightly

into a stance of assurance, and you allow
your hesitation to manipulate my stalk.

Your smallish pap sways back and forth
into a beam of moonlight.

When stroked, your strong hips undulate,
both bone and flesh,

at the crossroads of the animal ways.
The slag bag of your stomach

swings, contrarily to your tailbone.
Then the fragrance

of your great inland sea
fills the breeze in my soul.

Where the territories of two hunters overlap,
whether at mount or ravine,

along snake trails or at a cave mouth,
our hearts meet in the vast terrain

of a place only the sun, the moon,
and we can be.

Stripping Elderberries

This afternoon
beneath a shade tree
I stripped elderberries, lazily,
until my thumb
turned purple and funny.

Now, my wife, in a prickly mood,
stirs the black kettle
bubbling with jam
and a thousand seeds
to catch in my teeth.

A Wooden Cutout of an Old Woman's Backside

In Eden, Minnesota where County Road 16
slithers through the corn rows,

a painted image gives new homage
to the mysterious power of Mother.

In a garden beside the house
a rump stands bent near the lilies.

It's a cutout of wood, an irreverent wink
from granny's wild-ass nature.

This new country ritual shuns the bathtub Madonna
for an elderly arse in the berries.

My Wife Loading Her Cattle

Before 5 a.m. in late November
she stepped into the deep mouth of the trailer
and sweetly called to her cattle.
"Come on, boys. Look what I have for you."

Sniffing the metal and blackness before them
twin steers backed away from her beckon.
I squeezed a stall gate against the smaller one's ribs
'til he leaped toward her voice and went in.
"Good boy. Good boy."

The second steer turned and kicked on the pivot,
his brown bulk confused by her words.
He resisted the driver's twist of his tail
but finally had to jump into darkness.

"It's o.k., baby."
And his mother offered him corn.
The floor trembled, the trailer door slammed,
something rumbled in the muscles and meat.

My wife wept as her Cattle Boys left
to the Watkins Locker in Plum City.
She said nothing more, and neither did I,
then we both drove off to work.

In the Middle of an Argument

Sometimes, in the middle of an argument, a door flies open,
lightning flashes, and steely needles of rain begin to fall.
You feel as if you're in an open field,
unable to find a cave or a ditch.

Here, on the bluffs, where a log house
can be leveled by straight-line winds,
we've had practice dealing with storms.
If a hard wind gets inside,
the walls can fall, the roof rise and tumble,
and the debris piles on top
of the basement of fear and loneliness.

If I have to carry a plywood sheet
to nail over a broken window,
I carry it knife-like into the wind,
I walk sideways so the force won't throw me.

As I pull the door against the wind, it resists even more.
Then, at the instant when the door is edgewise
and I'm backing into the house,
I must take special care, make sure my fingers
won't get slammed to the jamb wood,
or the glass shatter over me.
I must resist the wind, just a bit,
push against it, and yield slowly
so we close the door together.

After the Battle

After the battle, after living in grief,
you smile at me, as sweetly
as flames from riven oakwood.

Your love, withheld for so long,
releases to warm me, with the scent
and fire of your hidden years.

From knots and gnarled heartwood
the fire burns hot and slow.
Just as grief derives from struggling,

and compassion is born from grief,
the face of holiness returns with you,
after the battle and the grief.

The Blizzard

At home we sit out the blizzard and wait two days
until the roads clear. Between chores we speak
of the neighbor's infidelities, incomplete affections, and how
humans cannot humanly fill all the needs of another.
We hold hands and scour one another's expectations.

What else can we do, except carry silences
behind hard lips with lines like
snow fences, and let our small wants
accumulate on top of one another,
the way drifts always pile up on the other side of the fence?

Tonight, the moon shines over the windwashed fields.
Tufts of unmown hay lift through the rippling whiteness,
like the body hairs we fondle after our boy goes to sleep,
like the holy promises we remember when we pray.

Not Naked on the Bed

Your beauty, nude
not naked on the bed,
is far more a gift
than I ever expected.
I watch languor recline
in your wise grey eyes
while slate hummingbirds
carved as earrings
dangle from golden hooks.
I quiver in your breath
and the ceiling fan halts
in that instant.
We look at one another
with both eyes open and close.
An intimate wind,
the cause of auroras,
moves north and south,
east and west,
then we swim
into one another.

Into My Quilts

Just as a bear goes down to its hole,
in winter I descend into my quilts.
My wife's arm warms my pillow
and the room is black
and comfortable this way.
Wrapped and curled
I'm a different being
with residual feelings from the day.

The warmth takes hold
of the irritations,
chattered gratitudes,
telephone static,
gasoline pump sounds,
and the radial tire-whines,
then melts them,
burns them away
like a cedar log snapping in the fire.

As I crawl deeper into my hole,
her warmth spreads through mine
and our two bodies, huddling
like slumbering badgers,
invite a mysterious third thing
into the welcoming dark.

In a harsh time— and one always comes—
fire explodes from tinder

and lightning,
although neither looks like a flame.
From ashes and soil
grow brilliant flowerheads,
and their perfumes waft unseen.
I don't know if my toe dreams
differently than my wife's ear, or
if our fingernails dream at all.
Yet something inside us knows.

My wife breathes
the same sleep rhythm as I.
No one else ever matched that rhythm.
It can't be an accident we sleep together.
Perhaps someone mysterious
waits inside our sleep,
and when we're asleep,
we're really awake.
The holy ones tell us,
"Such a being is there."

The Meditator in Love

Without your face
I would look onto the valley
and throw myself in—
like salt into sugar water
or smoke into fog.

And my life would end
without rapture,
and the coyotes
would chew my bones
to splinters, and lick out
my bloody marrow.

Without you
even my afterlife
would end,
miserably.

The Mystery Cave at Forestville

Women, whose breasts I wish to nuzzle,
and hips I yearn to lick, still sing into my sexual ear.
The faintest remainder of plum blossom scent
draws me toward the crevices of the smoothest danger.

It takes either great trust or foolhardy ignorance
to crawl into a cave which narrows
as if it were Lascaux with primal images,
or the Mystery Cave at Forestville.

Or to walk away, aching and relieved,
upright or crouched on a path through thorns and berries.
Either way, one must be prepared to get stuck,
and fail, and praise and delight.

Holy men may give contradictory words.
Holy women, too, stand on either shore.
But the blessing is not in the choice one makes
but in the constant movement in your heart.

Needin' Time

Come, sit in the cave behind my heart.
Without you, I'm empty.
Return once more, if only for moment,
we've not conversed enough, and I miss
your precious, silent presence.

3.

Inheritance

After I sledged the loosened stones
from the barn's crumbling foundation,
I had a hole, backfill rubble,
and house jacks cranked to the plate.

The wall hung like a hippo on tiptoe
as I repoured footings below the frostline.
When the concrete cures, although I'm a novice,
I'll mortar the blocks like a mason.

And as I carry those blocks to stack
by the barn, two by two by two,
my stiffening gait and weary arms
bend me toward the ground of my being.

Although he's napping on days like this,
I see my father in a window reflection,
beside me walking in a hat like mine,
and wearing my beard and moustache.

What We Wanted

I wanted my son to know
a hillside's green lap,
a darting goshawk,
the way pheasants bark,
and how your life grows
wider than your dream.

My wife wanted to tend,
again, a vegetable bed,
milk Alpine goats,
gather brown eggs,
then raise and ride
her many spirited horses.

Secretly, I wanted to live
as my grandfather did
before he left the prairie
to marry a city girl
in St. Paul, where he
lost so many good jobs.

Eventually, because he
rolled his own cigarettes,
because he drank port
and muscatel, because he
had blood clots and gangrene,
his riding legs were amputated.

From our farm, now,
I hear unfed cattle bellow
in our neighbor's stockpen.
And I see thunderstorms
approaching from the west
long before I want to.

The Strawberry Special

In the eastern night, one cloud is white,
like the back of my grandmother's head.
Her hair thin, her face averted,
waiting for the dawn, far away.

By her kitchen table Grandma sat in the city,
watching trains pull loads from the east.
Our house shook through her great silence
until the cars were west, and the earth still.

She'd tell the story of the Strawberry Special,
the rail spur she rode once in Dakota.
How she had to wait all night on the platform
at the station because the train couldn't make the incline.

An army of worms covered the tracks,
as writhing ribbons of grease.
At dawn beside her a dark tarpaulin shivered,
and a family of Sioux came out of their sleep.

When they continued, the caterpillars gone,
each leaf and grass blade had been devoured.
The Strawberry Special took her to her cousin,
and his pal, a cowboy with a buggy.

As an old woman she thrilled when her grandchildren squirmed
at this squeamish tale of her courtship.

Forty years later, I occasionally dream,
a locomotive is driving through my sleep.

The floors tremble, cattle cars shake,
power poles sway like bare saplings.
Then worms in the wall start to crawl through the cracks,
yet I awaken to a butterfly sunshine.

Why Some Women Discard Rattlesnake Skins

I
A young man mailed rattlesnake skins
from Dakota's razory grasses.
"These make great hat bands,"
he wrote to his sweetheart
in the East, in St. Paul,
"and no man should be without one."
She, a milliner, discarded them,
for she made women's hats
with great white plumes,
from the Everglade egret,
and silk flowers of brightly turned cloth,
which were sewn beside beads,
like sour, small berries.
Finally, the lace, like the wings of fairies,
could mask the hard eyes of the women.

II
Around the fire the old man danced
in a circle with a blanket
over his chilled, bony shoulders,
the holy muscatel heating his belly,
his story slept in his heart.
Under spiralling sparks,
in his grandson's gaze
a snake rose through the vines of blood.
As Grandma dealt solitaire

on her table at the window,
her head stringy white with psoriasis,
Gramps got stoned after seeing her glare,
then whispered before slumping on the ground,
"My great-granny was an Indian, and so are you."
Then he slept in his blanket by the fire.

III
I was awakened on a fur-lined blanket
by the sound of a cat on the glossy wood floor
in the apartment of a truck-driving woman.
"How wonderful" she told me
as I lay sultry and blurred,
"you trusted me enough to sleep . . . before me,
so sleep in my bed as long as you like."

When I Was Twenty

Grandpa leaned on his red hoe handle.
Beside the zinnias I saw his muscatel
and thought, "Damn, he'll play his harmonica
all night, and I have to study John Kenneth Galbraith."

The Thread of Sunlight

Where the thread of sunlight crossed the top bunk,
I touched the rough-cut rafter,
and watched two spiders approach
on the lumber's vertical plane.

Just when my heart condensed to arachnid size
the great wounds of war opened before me.
One spider limped on,
with the other's head in its mouth.

When I asked my mother about war,
she told me, "You're thinking too much and . . . "
Before her sentence ended my father rushed in,
chattering about the chores we'd accomplish.
The magneto for the mill saw needed repair,
the window trim should be painted,
the outboard motors could be tuned,
and if the work gets done,
we might go fishing in the evening.

The sunlight reflected off the flat lake
and I stood, between my mother
and my father, thinking.

Catching Up to the Words

If they had learned a melody, once,
my uncles and father remembered it
at a party, then galloped into song
one voice at a time, catching up
to the words.

And after my brother John's wake
they drank a little in the living-
room, with Uncle Jim's uninvited,
blubbering pal. I didn't know him.

I was nineteen, and angry,
and paced between the sink and the stove,
as the drunk babbled on and on and on.
Then Dad, then his brothers
came into the kitchen to talk
and get away from misery, one by one.

Small Duties

Some days my face relaxes
as if my grandpa's skin
folds over my cheekbones.
Animals don't smile with their faces,
and neither did grandpa.

Today, I have small duties ahead,
find a hummingbird feeder,
drive Daniel to a concert,
phone my godson, and ask how he's doing.

One dark peony is almost open,
and an old corn cob,
as dry as a rattlesnake tail
rests on the stoop in the sun.

The columbines droop,
and a hummingbird waits on the wire.
An old white oak tells me,
"A smile is not required."

From My Chair

I don't remember what dreaming I did last night,
yet today I'm quiet inside.
A split oak log burns away in the stove,
and a hard snow, like the rude world,
blows past my window.

My feet are warm,
and only my thoughts roam,
like boys to a party
where my Dad and uncles
sing Stephen Foster songs in harmony.

While they conjure a beautiful dreamer—
so contrary to their meat saws and power drills,
forklifts and card-party chatter—
a longing for quiet hides in their sentimentality.
Nothing ever frightened them more than silence.

I, too, know that fear well.
Yet because they found harmonious moments
in a woodshop, at Mass, or fishing at dawn,
I can sit alone, alert and quiet,
while my own boys run free in the world.

At Mesa Verde

On my lap in a white sleeping bag
Jess hears a high jet in the hollow night sky.
Like a prophet pointing to heaven
he looks first to me then bends back his face
and sees the storm of the stars.

I watch the moon rise,
and the campfire leaps in his eyes
as he sticks out his tongue
to catch a stardrop that falls
through the incense of
piñon and sage.

The Crickets

On waking in the darkness,
I thought my ears were ringing
from high blood pressure
I might have inherited.
Then, I thought, maybe,
it was a message from Grandma,
who, at 94, is trying to die.
Our world will resonate when she dies,
the way the earth does
when a fault line releases its strain.

Slowly, I recognized one cricket,
then another, and others.
It's as if something sent ahead
to warn us with their sound:
"A chill is coming
and a silence much deeper than night."

We Collect Gull Feathers

As the evening dies over Pepin,
we collect gull feathers, black and white ones,
and pretend they were dropped by the eagle
whose track and wing marked
the gray Mississippi sandbar.

Jesse remarked as we arrived,
"If I point at hawks they fly away,
but if I don't they stay in their trees."

The river moves heavily, south,
and the sun drops beyond the bluffs.
The air chills me.
I want to keep my fingers in my pocket,
because everything moves on here,
except that sweet pain of love that knows
he's growing up to leave me.

Prayer Cards in a Drawer

Near the power plant
eagles hang like despair
on the lip of river ice.
They eat the dead fish
that lift into open water.
The winds have turned
to warn the trees,
"A blizzard's coming.
The coldest days will follow."

Christmas approaches, and
my mother's mother prays to die,
because she can no longer eat.
Her mouth fills with purple sores, and
phlegm continues to rise in her throat.
She now keeps her teeth in a drawer
behind her prayer cards and courage.
And still death won't take her.

As I walk the town road in this, the darkest week,
hope hides in my deepest pocket.
I have trouble trying to pull it out
into December's low light.

Weeping for My Nephew *(even the moon's a red eye)*

During the last hour
the full moon grew smaller,
chewed by our shadow.
I've returned to my doorstep
after walking the pasture
and the snowfields.
On my snowshoe track,
snow-salmon swim
up the small drifts and ripples,
toward home.

Tonight, the moon is a red eye,
dying in a river of stars.
I've worked to a sweat
and with each breath,
I've prayed for my nephew
who fell from a ladder
and into a coma.
What light can guide him
as he wanders
the ocean inside himself?

This old moon is dying
in its birth stream,
as when a king,
a coho or humpback
struggle to get
back home

and I watch
the moon,
in tears,
sleepless,
and melancholy.

First Lessons

Spring blooms on warm Saturdays,
           twelve years old, and learning
the legal manner of shooting.

Prone position,
        .22 rifle,
                    ping. . . ping. . . ping,
a perfect shot,
        with a perfect understanding
                    of the laws.
He'll get his state certificate to hunt.

Autumn dries the soul,
            the woods,
and the leaves,
        which descend at their own time.
They drop away
            and heap in the wind
against a fallen, softened log,
        its oak-rot stinks
with sour, babyish wetness.

A gray squirrel scatters,
              chatters, then halts,
spreading upward on the grand river of bark.
        Its tail is as still as the grain in wood.

He shoots,
        the squirrel falls
                to the earth,
twitching,
        until he wrings its neck,
                as his father showed him.

While skinning the animal
he prefers the fur
to the pinkish carcass,
            doesn't like
      the wild smell,
but he learns,
        touches the pearly gray guts,
            the knee socket
      shaped like a flower,
and the deep red stains
        beneath the ribs.

Song in Praise of My Uncle's Death

God invaded his lungs with a vengeance,
    so he prayed,
   "This is too big for me,
     God, you take it."

An God, the diamond-back
    slid into the prairie dog holes
     to feast.

And God, the red-tail hawk
    swooped with Her talons of ice
     and punctured
    the slow gopher's skull
while it sniffed too far afield.

And God, the ravenous pike,
    darted through quivering reeds
     and snatched
    the black crappie whose dorsal fin
fought the mouth of teeth, and failed.

And God, the snake-tailed rat,
    crept through the sewer
      with Her eyes downturned
    for a future use.

HIS DAUGHTER ASKED,
"DAD, ARE YOU STILL WITH US?"

And God, the visible mist,
        smothered the landscape
                and ruined the picnic
        for the local clan.

And God, the Swift River,
        embraced the toddler
                who reached a crystal bridge
        at the spring thaw.

AND THE DAUGHTER ASKED A SECOND TIME,
"DAD, ARE YOU STILL WITH US?"

And God, the slippery hand,
        invaded his lungs
                with a vengeance.
        So he prayed.
"God, you take it, this is too big for me."

Geo ThirtyFive

TIMOTHY YOUNG lives in rural Wisconsin with his wife
and son and teaches juvenile offenders at the
Minnesota Correctional Facility in Red Wing. He is an
award-winning journalist and his essays and poems
have appeared in many national and local periodicals,
including *The Best American Poetry of 1999*.

Thanks

A great number of people have contributed to the publication of this book. I would like to especially thank my teacher and friend, Robert Bly who has inspired, aided and promoted my work. I would also like to thank the Minnesota Men's Conference and the men who funded the publication of this book. I also want to thank the teachers who have challenged me and my work with their intense love for living. They brought passion, delight and grief into my wooded homeland. Thank you, Martín Prechtel, Miguel Rivera, John Lee, James Hillman, Etheridge Knight, Haki Madhubuti, Aaron Kipnis, Robert Moore, Doug Von Koss, Willem de Thouars, Malidoma Some, Michael Meade, John Stokes, Terry Dobson, Onaje Benjamin, Richard Close, Lewis Hyde, Humberto Ak'abal, John Witherspoon, Matt Cohen, Craig Ng and Terrence Real. Thank you, Wick Fisher for your constancy. Thank you, Craig Ungerman, Mark Stanley and the Hidden Wine staff. Thank you, contributors, Ders Anderson, Jim Baecker, Scott Banas, Joel Carter, Tom Devine, Larry Fahnoe, Oral Fisher, Dennis Flom, Dennis Floyd, Lock Kiermaier, James LaSater, Bruce Lisiecki, Thomas L. Matthias, Jim Miller, Bob Roberts, Michael Simons, Alfred Thieme III, Jim Tifft, and Alan Zopf. I apologize for any forgotten names. Thank you, my fellow poets, Thomas R. Smith, Jay Leeming, Jim Dochniak, Tony Signorelli and Roy McBride. Thank you, my singing friends, David Ballman, Geoffrey Denison, Brad Fern, Tim Franzich, Kevin Gregerson, Sage Harmos, Glen Helgeson, Lanny Kuester, Bill McGaughey, Duncan Storlie, and Erik Storlie. Thank you, my fellow Cave Historians, Walton Stanley, David Gross, Kurt Meyer, David Schmit, Ed Groody, and Todd Davis. Thank you, my oldest friend, Sandy Morris. Thanks to my parents, all my brothers, sisters, nieces and nephews, aunts and uncles, grandparents and relatives whose lives I have used in my poems. Thank you, Divine Ones who help with my poems. Thank you, with all my love, Corrine, Jesse and Torleiv. Thank you, all unnamed, invisible or forgotten ones who contributed to the publication of this book.

TIMOTHY YOUNG
Stockholm, Wisconsin